POCKET

The Queen

WISDOM

POCKET
The Queen
WISDOM

Inspirational quotes
and wise words
from an iconic monarch

Hardie Grant

BOOKS

Pocket The Queen Wisdom

First published in 2018 by Hardie Grant Books,
an imprint of Hardie Grant Publishing
This edition published in 2022 by Hardie Grant Books,
an imprint of Hardie Grant Publishing

Hardie Grant Books (London)
5th & 6th Floors
52–54 Southwark Street
London SE1 1UN

Hardie Grant Books (Melbourne)
Building 1, 658 Church Street
Richmond, Victoria 3121

hardiegrantbooks.com

British Library Cataloguing-in-Publication Data. A catalogue
record for this book is available from the British Library.

ISBN: 978-1-78488-568-7
10 9 8 7 6 5 4 3 2 1

Publishing Director: Kajal Mistry
Design: Daisy Dudley
Illustrator: Michele Rosenthal
Production Controller: Katie Jarvis
Images on pages 7, 31, 55, 65, 75, 91 © Shutterstock

Colour Reproduction by p2d
Printed and bound in China by Leo Paper Productions Ltd.

Contents

The Queen on
LIFE

"

Grief is the price

we pay for

LOVE.

"

❝

[On her job] It's all to do
with the training: you
can do a lot if you're
properly trained.

❞

"

I know of no single formula
for **SUCCESS**.
But over the years I have
observed that some
attributes of leadership are
universal and are often
about finding ways of…

encouraging people
to combine their efforts,
their talents, their insights,
their enthusiasm and
their inspiration to

WORK
TOGETHER.

"

66

When life seems hard,
the courageous do not lie down
and accept defeat; instead,
they are all the more determined
to struggle for a better future.

99

"

Let us not take ourselves too
seriously. None of us has
a monopoly on wisdom and we
must always be ready to listen and
respect other points of view.

"

"

May you be **PROUD** to remember – as I am myself – how much depends on you, and that even when your life seems most monotonous, what you do is always of real **VALUE** and importance to your fellow men.

"

"

The true measure
of all our actions is how
long the **GOOD** in
them lasts.

"

"

We can make sense
of the future, if we
understand the lessons
of the past.

"

"

The world is not the most
pleasant place. Eventually
your parents leave you and
nobody is going to go out
of their way to protect you...

unconditionally. You need to learn to stand up for yourself and what you believe and sometimes – pardon my language –

KICK SOME ASS.

,,

66

Work is the rent
you pay for the room
you occupy on earth.

99

"

In tomorrow's
world we must all

WORK

TOGETHER

as hard as ever.

"

"

It has always been easy
to hate and
DESTROY.
To build and to
CHERISH
is much more difficult.

"

"

Today we need a special kind of courage. Not the kind needed in battle, but a kind which makes us stand up for everything we know is right.

"

"

It is possible to have too
much of a good thing.

"

"

I hope we will all be

reminded of the

POWER

of togetherness and the

convening strength of

FAMILY,

friendship and good

neighbourliness.

"

66

There are long periods
when life seems a small,
dull round, a petty business
with no point, and then
suddenly we are caught up...

in some great event,
which gives us a glimpse
of the solid and durable
foundations of our

EXISTENCE.

"

"

GOOD MEMORIES

are our second

chance at

HAPPINESS.

"

"

For me,

HEAVEN

is likely to be a bit
of a come-down.

"

The Queen on

SOCIETY

"

[After 9/11]
My thoughts and
prayers are with you all
now, and in the difficult
days ahead.

"

"

[When a businessman's phone rang as he was speaking to the Queen] Why don't you answer that? It might be someone important.

"

"

We all need to get the
balance right between
action and reflection.
With so many
distractions, it is easy
to forget to pause and
take stock.

"

"

It has been

WOMEN

who have breathed

gentleness and

CARE

into the hard progress

of mankind.

"

"

In the modern world the
opportunities for women
to give something of value to the
human family are greater than
ever, because, through their own
efforts, they are now beginning
to play their full part in public life.

"

"

There can be no doubt,
of course, that

CRITICISM

is good for people and
institutions that are part
of public life.

"

" TRUE PATRIOTISM

doesn't exclude an understanding of the patriotism of others.

"

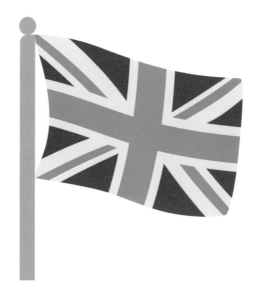

"

The lessons from the

PEACE

PROCESS

are clear; whatever life

throws at us...

our individual responses
will be all the stronger for

WORKING
TOGETHER

and sharing the load.

,,

"

Let us set out to build
a truer knowledge
of ourselves and our fellow
men to work for tolerance and
understanding among the…

nations and to use the
tremendous forces of science
and learning for the
betterment of man's lot
upon this earth.

"

"

The upward course
of a nation's history is
due in the long run to the

SOUNDNESS
OF HEART

of its average men
and women.

"

"

With the benefit of

HISTORICAL

HINDSIGHT

we can all see things

which we would

wish had been differently

or not at all.

"

"

The decisions we make should always be designed to enlarge their [the young's] horizons and enrich their future, from caring for our environment to preventing conflict.

"

"

All of you, near
or far, have been
UNITED
in one purpose.

"

"

The

BRITISH

constitution has always been

PUZZLING

and always will be.

"

"

It is not the new
inventions which are the
difficulty. The trouble
is caused by unthinking
people who carelessly
throw away ageless ideas
as if they were old and
outworn machinery.

"

"

FOOTBALL IS A DIFFICULT BUSINESS

and aren't they

prima donnas?

"

"

1992 is not a year on
which I shall look back
with undiluted pleasure.
In the words of one of my
more sympathetic
correspondents, it has
turned out to be an
annus horribilis.

"

"

[Speaking to Eric
Clapton at a Buckingham
Palace reception in 2005]
Have you been playing
a long time?

"

The Queen on
FAMILY

"

Family does not necessarily
mean blood relatives,
but often a description
of a community,
organisation or nation.

"

"

Like all the best families,

we have our share of

eccentricities, of impetuous and

WAYWARD

YOUNGSTERS

and of family disagreements.

"

"

First, I want to pay tribute
to Diana myself. She was an
exceptional and gifted human
being. In good times and bad,
she never lost her capacity to
smile and laugh, nor to inspire…

others with her warmth and kindness. I admired and respected her – for her energy and commitment to others, and especially for her devotion to her two boys.

99

"

[On Diana]
I, for one, believe there
are lessons to be drawn
from her life and
from the extraordinary
and moving reaction
to her death.

"

66

If I am asked what
I think about family life
after 25 years of

MARRIAGE,

I can answer with equal
simplicity and conviction,
I am for it.

99

"

It's the

SECRET

of a happy marriage to

have different

INTERESTS.

"

"

These wretched

BABIES

don't come until

they are ready.

"